Liam McCormick is a poet who w
know. He left the Black Isle at six
since had work featured on BBC
as part of the match build-up t
He has supported acts such as K
Johnson. He is now a writer and performer living in Glasgow.

This is his first saga.

Beast

Liam McCormick

Burning Eye

BurningEyeBooks
Never Knowingly
Mainstream

This edition published by Burning Eye Books 2018

www.burningeye.co.uk

@burningeyebooks

Burning Eye Books
15 West Hill, Portishead, BS20 6LG

ISBN 978 1 911570 26 4

THIS IS

A BOOK

ABOUT LOVE

We follow Zara as she rants and raves her way through Glasgow's gig economy. When the Council pilot a red-light district in the Merchant City, she realises she could have it so much better. Fuelled by fantasies of fame and fortune, Zara runs as fast as she can from the past which stalks her like a crazy ex-boyfriend.

Scotland's rising poetic star takes on rape culture. Cheeky, provocative and gut-wrenching, this book is an intense portrait of the cycle of abuse. Written with intense anger, throbbing tension and serene release - BEAST is an essential text for those wishing to challenge toxic masculinity.

For
Lou, Jo and Cee.

Spells written by Catherine Smith

Cover by Ella Russel

Art by Mark Penrose

Design by Bram E Gieben / Weaponizer Press

Thanks to Rebecca, Leanne, Audrey, Dad, Jiggles and Zahra,
for giving me a place to sleep while I wrote this book.

Thanks to Aimee,
for letting me rant Zara into existence.

Thanks to Extra Second Glasgow and Inn Deep Poetry,
for letting me try out new material.

Thanks to Louie,
for showing me how its done.

Thanks to Planet Earth
for all of the plants and animals,
to Time
for healing all wounds ,
and to Jacob.

CONTENTS

PART 3: WEED

1. A SHORT POEM ABOUT LOVE BY ME

this   looks

more   like   an

arse   than

a   heart

fuck

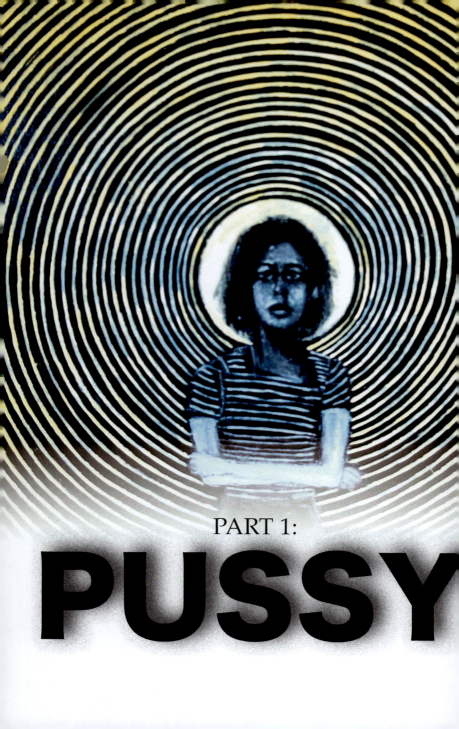

PART 1:
PUSSY

2. ZARA GETS READY FOR A NIGHT OUT

–You can tell everything you need to know about a man by what he describes as *beautiful*. If he says it about everything he's a pussy. If he doesn't say it at all he's a cock. If he claims not to be either he is a liar.

sniff sniff

fuckin…

coughing fit

Listen. If you want to start a club night, and you want it to keep going, and you want it to be banging, here is what you do:

sniff

Invite as many hot girls as you can. Instagram has made this once-difficult step as simple as tapping your fingers on a desk. Any other hot girls that walk up? In for free. When they're on their way out get them on Facebook. If the drugs they brought are good enough this should be easy. If the drugs they brought aren't good enough, make sure you've got someone on the floor punting good pills. When they come back let them in for free. If they've brought pals.

sniff sniff

Obviously the tunes have to be beautiful.

coughing fit

3. ZARA'S MOTHER TEXTS HER TELLING HER TO REMEMBER TO HAVE FUN

get home safe
gethomesafe   gethomesafegethomesafe
gethooomesafegethooomesafegethoomesafe
gethomesafe   ho   fe   hom   e
get home safe   me   safe
                                        get

do not leave your drink
unattended do not le
ave your   0   drink
unatten 0 ded do
not leav 0 e you
r drink O   un
attended do

4. ZARA NECKS A SHOT AS THE WEASEL SIDLES UP

–Y'know.
The Bucky mingles with the blood
As the blood with the communion,
The winds of heaven mix for ever,
With a sweeter kind of union,
No malt in the bar is single,
All measures by a law we define,
In one spirit meet and mingle,
Why not yours with mine?

Zara tells him she's gonny take a pish.

–I don't think you understand.
See the magpies kiss the cladded high rise
As the lovers inside grasp one another,
No sister floo'er would be alive
If it disdained its brother,
And the lamplights grasp the earth,
And the moonbeams kiss the Clyde,
What is all this sweet work worth,
If thou kissed not I?

She killed him with a look.

5. ZARA IS PULLED AWAY FOR AN INTENSE CONVERSATION IN THE LADIES' TOILET

Love loves working too much.
Love loves borrowing money.
Love loves taking up all your time.
Love loves not texting back.
Love loves drinking until it's sick.
Love loves changing plans.
Love loves coming home late.
Love loves cockroaches.
Love loves cumming too quickly.
Love loves not cumming at all.
Love loves snoring.
Love loves asking for head in the morning before it's even washed its fanny.
Love loves smoking in bed.
Love loves crying.
Love loves arguing.
Love loves getting what it wants.

But love is in love
Because love loves love. So love
Is in love with love.
Zara yawns.

Sarah explains:
Love is like sleeping in a warm bath.
It's dangerous, but worth it.
The steady pace,
The uneven float,
The loosened muscles,
The growing stomachs,
O, how I have revelled in the binges of love.

Zara snorts:
–Patch that!
Who wants to be the cunt that drowned in their own bath?

6. ZARA'S ARSE IS BITTEN BY THE DOG

Sinking rums and bedding ones,
Chewing blues and grooving twos,
Ketamine keys and kissing threes,
Smoking scores and scoring fours,
Saving lives and pulling fives,
Banging mixes and banging sixes,
Manna from heaven
When I winch a seven.
Paying mates' rates tay
Fornicate way eights,
Sniffing lines and shagging nines,
Sipping glens and nipping tens.

Drinking Mad Dog and
Pumping your Maw.

7. STALKER

On the 17.54 ScotRail service from Inverness to Kyle of Lochalsh.

You have your hood pulled up. Zoned out. You don't see me. But I seen you. You get off at the Muir. I get off at the Muir.

I walk proud. Head. High. Shoulders. High. Heels. Kicking. Up. Dust. I look unrecognisable.

As you walk under the overpass I get the feeling you know someone is watching you. But round here everyone knows everything about everybody. You probably feel like someone is watching you a lot. I hope you feel like someone is watching you a lot.

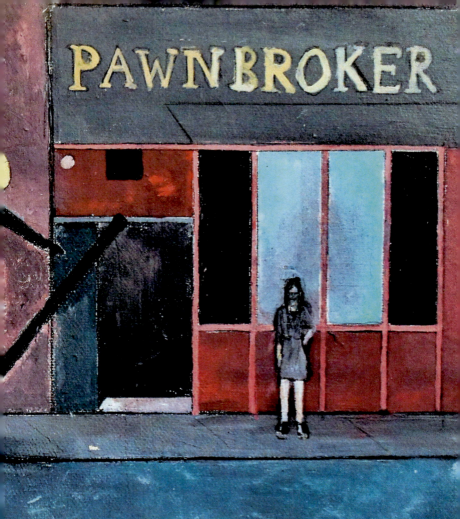

You cut by the park and I remember the day we met.

My teeth grit. I mutter I love you under my breath. I try to stuff the I love you's back in my mouth. You reach your front door, fumble with the keys and let yourself in. I wait for an hour before I leave.

8. ZARA MEETS A DUCK

Mirror, mirror on the wall,
Who's the baddest cunt of them all?
Leering, staring. Sneer ensnaring,
See me glaring like a soul bearing balls.

Clean sambas with the mirror toe-caps,
Best seat in the house for checking out
Her pout and snatch.

Above the mirror there is a sign saying:

DON'T RAPE

Eh, wasn't planning on it, mate.

Step out the toilet,
Check out the talent,
Clock three hotties:
She's maybe a quarter past me,
She used to be a 9 but big hand is closing in on 55,
She's off her face but out my league.

I twist my head like another Corona and lime,
There's a boy looking at me, one, two, three, four times.

But by a gracious god's will!
We are both coming up
On the exact same pills!

It must be love.

–See, if I was a woman, I think I'd be you but the same.
–If I was a man I'd be Putin.
–I've always wanted a woman to help me—
–WHAT?
–I SAID I'VE ALWAYS WANTED A LASSY TO HELP ME
RETAKE THE UKRAINE.

Beat her eardrum with the wind from my tongue.
She's sexy but not effortlessly. She dances to have fun.
We've got chemistry like ket and mandy.

It must be love.

Twist my head like another Corona and lime,
That boy is still looking at me one, two, three, four times.

Break sweat, make a bet, place a cigarette
Between her lips. She nods her hips.
Reveals her wit in the smoking bit while I

chat shit.

–Check they fuckin ducks, man!

Five actual ducks waddle past the club.

–That one reminds me of you.
–How?
–Its feathers are different from the rest. It's a bit farther away
from the others. It looks like it might feel lonely sometimes. But
I think the reason the mum duck lets it wander is because she
knows it can handle itself. Its life will be that bit more exciting,
more special for it.

Then I'm grinding her ass like it's my teeth.

Twist my head like another Corona and lime,
That boy is still looking at me one, two, three, four times.

Lights coming up soon like a lunatic's full moon.

–You got an afters sorted?
–You don't?
–Was planning having cunts up at mine.
–I suppose you'll want to take me back and when no one turns

up we'll have to make our own fun.
–Eh?
–Or you'll want to come wherever I'm going, and when we
come down and realise we don't have anything in common
you'll spend the rest of the night following me around until I
get uncomfortable and crash in my friend's bed.
–Hey hey hey, I'm not going to pretend you didn't catch my
eye. Aye, I don't know you, but, girl, I want to show you the
respect the world owes you. I think we've found common
ground surrounded by the sounds and beat. I just want to see
if the heat is proximity or if you are honestly that sweet.
–You got weed?

Bitch.

I smoked the last of the hash in a broken caste,
Tied my tales to the sails of a sinking ship's mast,
Then I weathered a storm like I don't know I'm born,
I was torn between themes of schemes and dreams,
But leaning on teen queens fiending green leaves
Leaves me obscene,
                    but fuck it
                              am keen.

Twist my head like another Corona 'n' lime,
That boy is still looking at me one, two, three, four times.

He looks like a rent boy.
If he is he's unemployed,
'Cause his coke cock is like The Rock's is
After ten years of jagging steroids.

–What did you say your name was?
–Sarah.

Danger? I cause it.
He's a wee prick,

I make sick chicks vomit
On my thick dick.

–You get your coat. I'll meet you outside.

Reverse out and rev the engine,
In the hands of a drunk the wheel is a weapon,
And this cunt's got the same intention,
Aggression probably wants the bird I'm necking.
I growl and prowl.   He growls and prowls.
My eyes flare.   His eyes flare.

       –Awrite? ¿etirwA

Thrust my nut ready for scrap he's bringing to me,
Crash,   metal twists   stung   lash
Glass   sticks to my forehead.

The lights come up.

Above the shattered mirror there is a sign saying:

              DON'T RAPE
    my enemy
              was a mirror…
     …fuck…
         …Sarah…
    …let's fuckin…
           …fucked it.

Walk me   home, lasssssy, ho   me.   A   nd
        we'll all walk home the   gither.
    Throw a   wild   par   ty at mi
ne.
  'Cus that   taxi queue s for   ever.

23

oooo

ah

ooooo   ah

up the

ra.

9. ZARA GOES TO AN AFTERPARTY

y'know when you're at an afterparty but it's the afterparty of
an afterparty of an afterparty of an afterparty and every cup
is an ash tray so you go to the cupboards but all there is is one
pint of milk that developed sentience two weeks ago, and you
start wishing for a jumper because the central heating hasn't
been turned on since the council tax got paid (never), and
you're only wearing a sweat-soaked T-shirt and your kidneys
hurt and you spent so long pretending to text someone that
your phone died and then this tune comes on

rrrr-rrr-rrr-rrr-rrr-rrr-rrrr-rrr-rrr-rrr-rrr-rrr-rrrr-rrr-rrr-rrr
THIS   IS   YOUR   WORST   NIGHTMARE!

Werewolves full of the tune chew,
And take turns to gurn at the moon.
They are wired to.

Half cut like a cosmonaut,
Trying to untie Alexander's knot
On a space walk. I've got

Rock stars in my eyes like cataracts.
Small-town heroes on zero-hour contracts
Have the ambition to pass the bam audition,
But the gram got was bought by their mam,
Like their education.

Suddenly a scuba diver
Jumped out a pint of cider,
Says he found a treasure map that'll
Get you inside her.

In the virgin–whore dichotomy I'm obviously
More of a Magdalene than Madonna.
Think silk, I'm as righteous as Christ is,

25

Drink milk, I pish human kindness.

In space no one can hear you scream
HAS ANYBODY GOT ANY BACCY?

Then a weather witch produced a pouch,
Sat me down, spelled it out,
Handed me a spell book to help me out.

–But my itchy bits are sitting on a nervous breakdown!
She told me – Icarus
                lit a joint
                    off her wings
                            as
                    s
                     he
                            c
                              a
                               m
                                e
                            d
                             o
                              w
                              n
                               .
                                .
                                .
                               j
                                u
                                 s
                                  t
                                 h
                            a
                             v
                             i
                             n
                            g

```
                a
                  m
                     o
                       m
                       e
                       n
                       t
J                                     T
U    \justhavingamoment/              N
  S      \thavingamome/               E
  T      \sthavingamo/                M
  H      \havdealing/                 O
  A      \einwitha/                   M
  V      \myour/                      A
  I      \jshita/                     G
  N         \ju/                      N
_____

  N          / s \                    N
  G         / t  \                    I
  A        / h    \                   V
  M       / a      \                  A
  O      / v        \                 H
  M     /    i       \                T
  E    /      n       \               S
  N   /justhavingamoment\             U
TNEMOM  A  GNIVAH  TSUJ
```

10. ZARA WHITEYS

Give everything to me.

You never loved me.

I overhear the side-eye
from the passers-by when I try
passing off schlock about my pussy
and my cock.

> VIRGIN
> VIRGIN
> VIRGIN
> VIRGIN

You adorned me with antlers.

You chose
To not
Give me
Every
>> ounce
>> grain
>> whole

All you gave me was crocodile tears for phantom pain.

11. ZARA GETS HER SECOND WIND

Zara has a passport that could kick a Pegasus's ass.
Zara has a flat that stinks of blessedness and grass.
They tried to sell her 1.9 brats, getting fat,
And never paying a mortgage back,
But she patched that chat and now
She's holier than thou twats.
Because the room she lives in has every world religion's
Luxury tourist trap prayer mats.

Zara has a drug dealer saved on her phone as 'Instagramz'.

Zara has a business which is none of yours.
She's a private girl, dressed in pearl, she
Walks and talks like money, honey.

She's done her 10,000 hours of practice
On the matters of patter, poise and slapstick.
She draws eyes like artists don't really,
Because there's no way she would ever do it for free.

Zara has a loop pedal with her asking 'what is love' in eight
parts of harmony.

She's heard the slurs that men in clubs
With mirrored shoes
Gargle with marvel,
But to her they're the same sounds the stuck-up use.

That dress fits her like a balloon fits air.
That dress fits her like a note fits her nose.
That dress fits her like a cock fits her arse.

Practises Muay Thai on the thoughts that sting her,
Catches an evil eye on her middle finger,
Breaks her zen to tell them –Don't worry, hen! I don't steal
men; I fucking eat them.

Zara has a clock that counts the minutes backward from thirty.

When Sarah was halfway dead, her mother said:
–Athletes'll make ye greet, date doctors instead.
Sound advice, so Sarah ignored them,
Till she found tears forming,
Not by heartbreak, but by boredom.
The self-proclaimed intelligentsia
Were never very intelligible to her,
Wording over trips looking her arse over tit.
COME ON, NICE GUYS! She's not a fucking idiot.

If Zara was a pornstar she'd call herself Sylvia Gash.

Zara went to the butcher's the other day.
Through the peeled fat and bloody flesh,
She saw Sarah in a state of undress.
She asked for a slice off the stomach,
A cutlet from the calf, no, no chicken fillets.

Zara switched off her gear fear stare again.
The butcher's wide eye winked and said,
–I know how you feel, hen: I'm a vegetarian.

Zara has a mama with that ambition.

She told her the only difference between an artist and a
businessman
Is the businessman knows that rumours say more about the
people spreading them than the people they are about.

Her mother washed every dish she ever ate off,
Her mother always paid door charge on her night off,
Because she never had to wait too long.
But Sarah's seen her watching clocks,
Counting tick-tocks and grey locks.
Eyelashes fall off, and she wishes
For nothing but her daughter's happiness.
But Zara wears fake lashes.
Because the difference between a plan and a dream
Is knowing what the fuck you are doing.

12. ZARA WALKS HOME AT 9 AM WITHOUT A JACKET

A Spell for Rain

Lean in.

Blink often.

Keep your mouth together.

Laugh and sing.

You can't get any wetter.

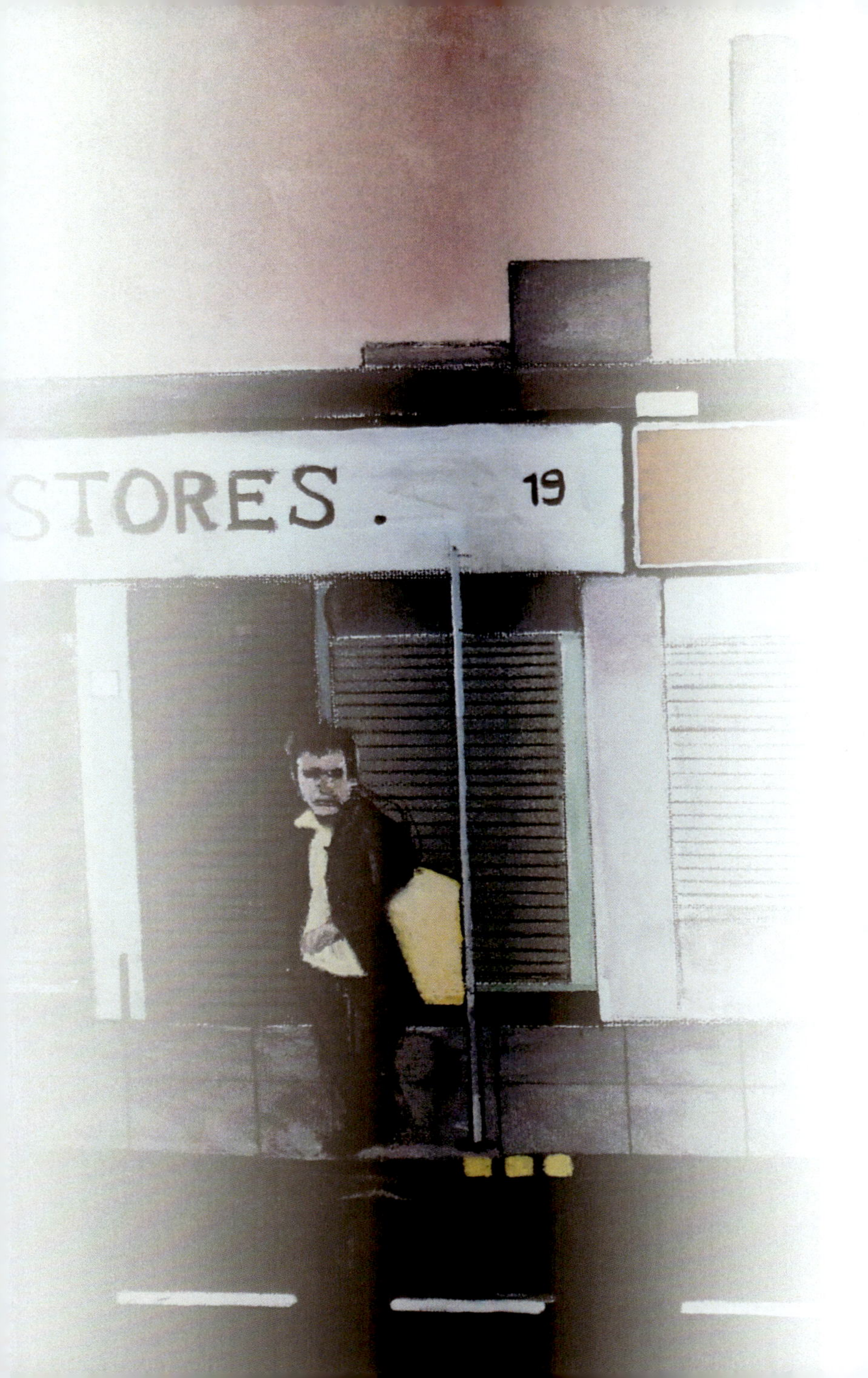
STORES.
19

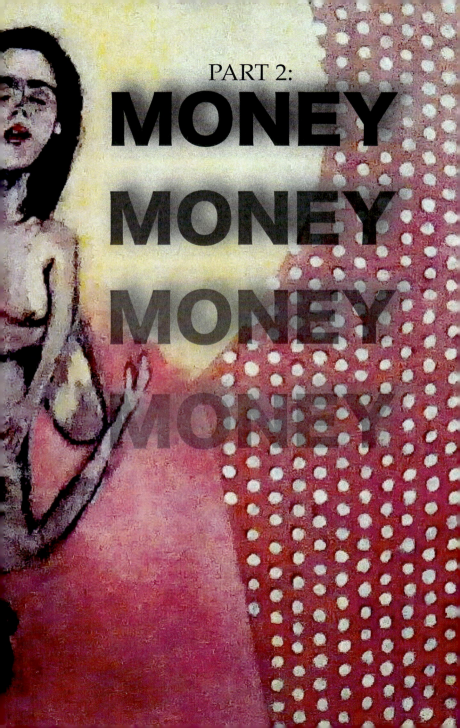

PART 2:

MONEY

MONEY

MONEY

MONEY

13. ZARA GETS THE NUMBER 38 BUS TO WORK

–It's just no right.

Nobody acknowledges him. Nobody makes eye contact.
Everybody still has to listen.

–With all these diversions we'd be better getting a 57 and then
jumping a train at Queen Street.[1] They've added a half-hour
on the route from Vicky Road[2] to Dennistoun.[3] And for what?
So bloody Montgomery King can fill the toon up with hoors?
It's a bloody disgrace. Back in wur day[4] you fell in love, and
you stayed in love.[5] Good times and bad, know? Paying for
it, oh, that was for scum and only scum. For dirty bastards
that didny know how to love a woman. I used to stay in the
Gorbals,[6] sure. I know what those Kings are all about. Bloody
gangsters ra lotta them. That company the boy runs? You know
the boy, Poofy[7] Wee[8] Monty? Aye, see his company? That
C1? Built aff the back of his daddy's dodgy dealings. They
run Guard Force Security. GFS,[9] that security mob that do all
the big gigs, fitba games and dancings and that. Gangsters
are running the doors! It's a fuckin joke! Now Glezga[10] is just
gonny sit back and let that shower punt poor wee lassies'
you-know-whats to Christ-knows-who? Selling them out of
shop windows! The Merchant City used to be the economic
engine of this country. A monument to the best we can make

---

1 Chisolm Street
2 King Road
3 Merchant City East
4 Back when you could legally rape your wife
5 Citation needed
6 New Gorbals
7 Effete in a manner which indicates homosexuality or wealth
8 Small either in relation to another person of the same name, or to
indicate the subject is diminutively connected to a third higher-status
party
9 Police Scotland
10 Glasgow

ourselves. Now it's a den of hoors and gangsters.[11] No even real gangsters. Where's the Arthur Thompsons? Where's the Jimmy Boyles? Where's the Matt Lygates? If they were here today they would probably be experimental techno DJs or some such shite. And their weans are still here. Still making their dodgy dealings. Still swanning about like they own the fucking place. But now they're doing it in the City Chambers.[12] Comfy and connected affy Daddy's success.

It's like animals getting married. Starts off all innocent. Just a laugh. Two dugs have a litter, and they say, aw, they've had kids, let's get them married! Dead cute. Then one day they come in with a dug and a cat that live together. They get on, which is even cuter becausy the natural animosity between dugs and cats. They're lit aht-aw, let's get them married! They're basically doing it together already, what's wrong with having it out in the open? Then before you know it BOOM! Monty King is baw deep in a staffy.

---

11 It has always been exactly that
12 The Glasgow Stock Exchange

14. ZARA GETS OFF AT LIDL AND WALKS

The Riverboat floats like a bad joke,
Where back meets knife,
On the very waters
That gave Glasgow
Life.

The cathedral isn't the only needle,
And the guilt isn't just Catholic.

Statues' eyes are downcast in shame,
On the square that keeps a secret in its name.

Cross the Kingston bridge.
Walk up Jamaica Street.
On the four corners,
You will find
The backs we build on now.

REMEMBER:

If it was built wi' stanes
Then it was built bi' slaves.

But one day, soon,
I pray,
The glass and chrome
Will be made to atone.

Wage slaves make Glasgow.

15. ZARA LOOKS IN A CAFÉ AND CATCHES A MAN'S EYE FOR LITERALLY TWO SECONDS

She stares at me as if from a window.
Coffee and cream between her
Lips.
I try to avert my eye but the gaze
Is met in the mirror. Look deeply,
Deeply. Yes, I am hungry.

The waitress brings me a full breakfast.

–Mumma's cooking for hungry boys!

As I eat the chef stares as if behind a hidden camera.
Hot, thick, covered in cream.
With every bite and lick my appetite grows.
Pussy on a plate, I look deeply,
Deeply. Yes, I am hungry.
The desire rises like a hard wet cock.
Do I want juice? a coffee? a fag? a drink? a joint? an eccy? a
jelly? a rock of crack?

I want women's lib for horny boys.

16. STALKER

I knew you were in. It was the low glow from the TV that gave you away. And the bathroom light switching on and off and on and off.
I've done a lot of waiting. Waiting for busses. Waiting for the rain to stop. Waiting for dealers to turn up. I've learned to like waiting.

Time doesn't really exist, only the measurement of time. And we are bad at measuring time. We go through it second by agonising second.

But how quickly it goes when it's too late.

17. ZARA THINKS THE SEAGULLS ARE LAUGHING AT HER

HAHAHA   HAHAHA
   HA   HA
   HA   HA
  HA   HA
   HAHA

      HAHAHA   HAHAHA
        HA   HA
        HA   HA
       HA   HA
       HAHA

HAHAHA   HAHAHA
   HA   HA
   HA   HA
  HA   HA
   HAHA

      HAHAHA   HAHAHA
        HA   HA
        HA   HA
       HA   HA
       HAHA

      HAHAHA   HAHAHA
        HA   HA
        HA   HA
       HA   HA
       HAHA

HIGH STREET

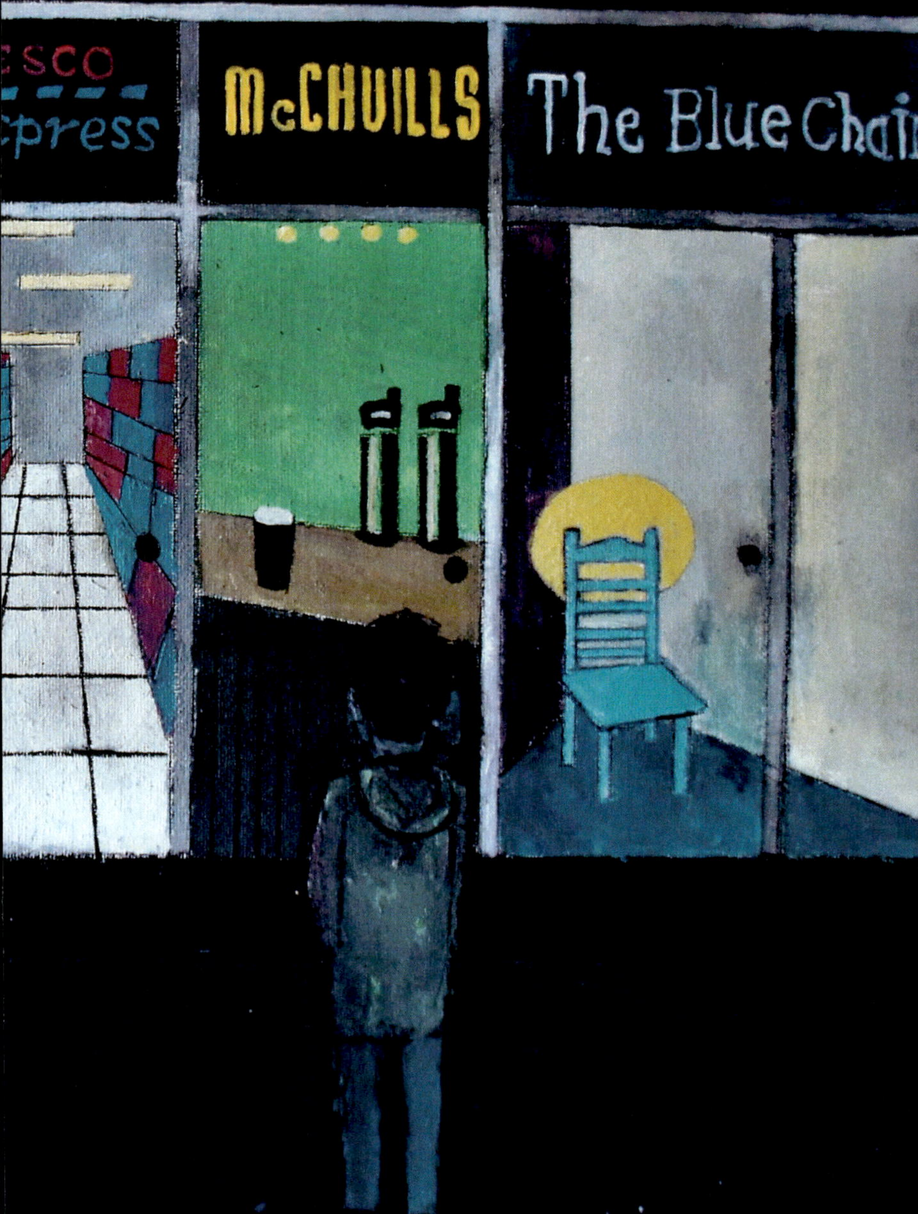

ESCO
Xpress
McCHUILLS
The Blue Chai

18. ZARA GOES THROUGH THE MOTIONS

A rabbit in the red lights
Is refracted back on the moist glass,
As I eye the attractions
That are tip-tap-tapping.

I go round and round the merry-go-round,
My eyes swipe right over every sight to see,
I always worry there might be
Something hornier round the corner.

Then Goddess opens her window.
Grabs my arm, smiles and says she knows.

–Hiya, big boy. You like?

I step ham-footed in.
My words jangle like keys.
But she, professionally,
Puts me at ease.

–What's your name?

–Eh… Scott.

–Where are you from?

–Scotland.

–Big strong farmer boy
wants to come fuck the city girls, eh?

–Where are you from?

Her eyes flash away for a liar's moment.
And she says Glezga the same way I do.

–I've never done this before. Well, no, like, I've had sex, just
never done it with a prosti— eh, um, eh, it's just I've never had
it with a sex worker.

This boy has never had a ride in his life.

She asks me how old I am,
And leads me by the hand
Down the tunnel-cum-corridor
That ends at a bed.

The floor reminds me of grit in my teeth.
Like a swimming pool changing room,
Easy to hose down, rinse and repeat.
The boudoir smells like perfume

That was bought by the gallon.

The bed has no blankets.
I sit on the edge.
Like I did the night
She left.

        I am shite at small talk. But I understand cock.
          Every cock has a certain way it sees itself,
        That does not match the man it's attached to.

She slides my coat off my back,
Rubs my shoulders and asks
If I'm a manual labourer.
She smooths my long hair down,
Which I puffed out like a chest,
From not being able to cope

With stress…

        –This is a working man's haircut.

–What's your name?

        –Zara.

–That's not your name, is it?

I get the scent of sweat drip-dripping,
my back, sack and crack,

pits swimming.
I hand over fifty pound.
She eases my trousers down.

                    Fucking hell, his balls are stinking.

I wish I'd shaved my cock.
It looks a lot bigger when I shave it.
She puts my dick in a bagel-shaped napkin.
Puts the condom on me.
I can feel those weird hairs that grow, like,
halfway up my shaft chafing against the latex.

            −You are beautiful.

        The space between their lips where they should kiss
            Fills with mist as they exhale exaltations.

        Like a turtle on its back he lies defenceless,
    The earth sloped off her shoulders but she hasn't noticed it.

    They beg to spill the secrets that'll sink their own ships.
    This is my submission. My rebirth. My kingdom of heaven.

I am hers. I am hers. I am hers.

                    He has definitely never had a blow job
                            this good   before.

For a moment.

She takes the condom off.

I put my clothes back on.
Thank her.

Walk out the corridor.
Let myself out the window.

As I walk back up High Street,
I pass a festival of red lights.
I want to see her again,
But when I look back,
I can't remember which window was hers.

My willy feels wet, and tingling.
I've never had an orgasm on my feet.
Never wanted a cuddle
In the middle of a busy street.

In each body I see a tapestry
As rich as the universe's history.

A thousand minds living lives
Just as important as mine.

In the battle between self-care
And conscious conduct I switch sides.

But the love I feel for a perfect stranger
Shows me there are more stars in heavens
Than just the sun.

I don't like the customers.
I don't like the hours.
I don't like my boss.
I like being the best at something.

Sex is like poetry.
Your own is the best you will ever know.

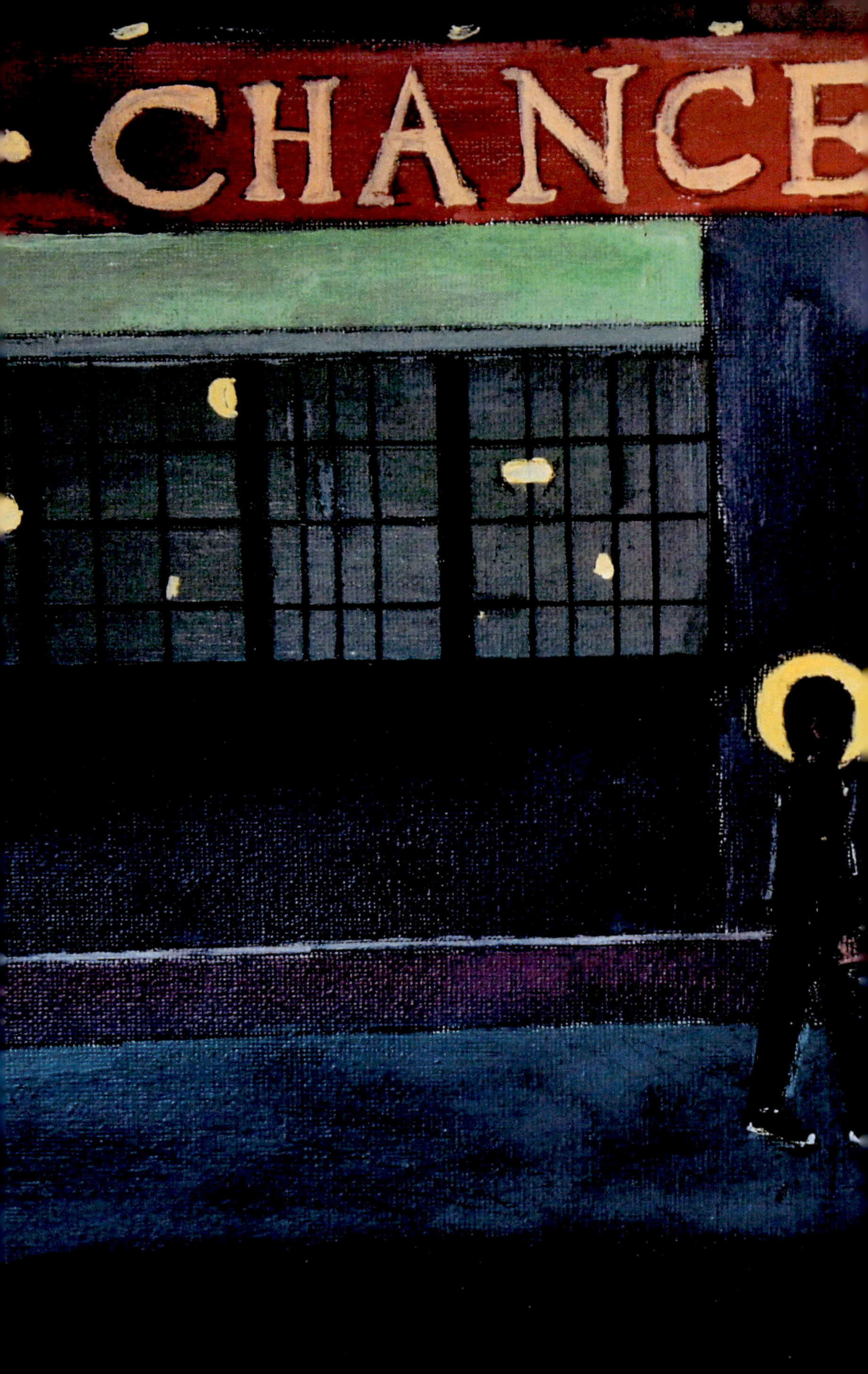
CHANCE

The Spell of History

Find the women guiding every movement

THEY

Are the Revolution

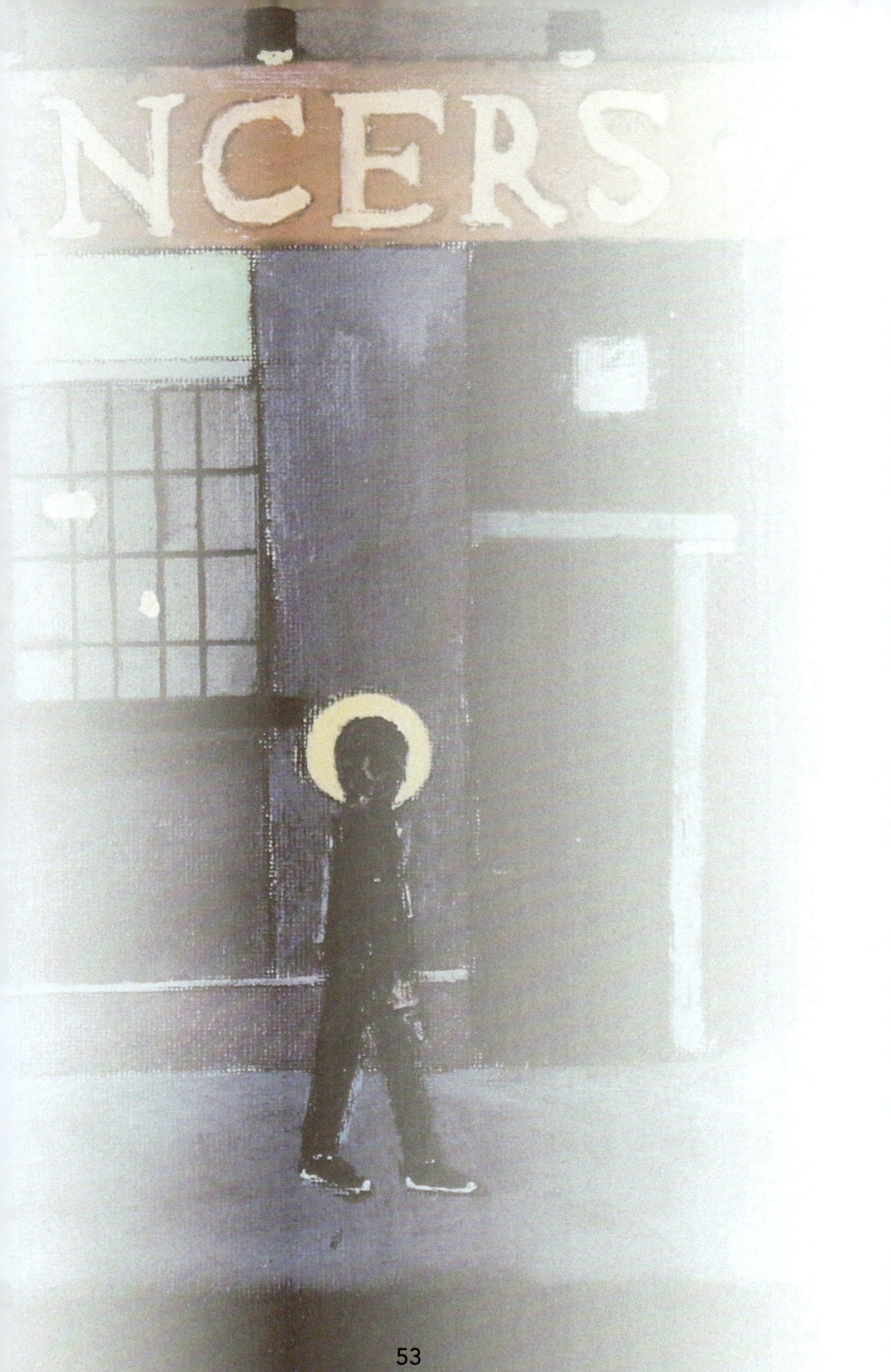
NCERS

FANNY MERCHANT

20. ZARA'S BOSS IS AN ARSEHOLE

My father lies face-down on his bed, knees resting on the floor, while a bitter hag wipes his bum. I can hear him mumbling. He's asking me to get Ava. I would tell him that Ava is dead, but I'd just have to tell him again in a couple of hours. The nurse asks me to put his dirty nappy in the bin. I wrinkle my nose, look down at my iPhone and hear her trudge away.

A man should never have to look at his father's drooping buttocks. But we are the men that can do what all the others cannot.

When I had just graduated from the prestigious St Aloyisius' College, my father took me to the Gorbals. Though I suppose it's the Old Gorbals now. His Rolls-Royce rolled slow around his old scheme, waving at every old face. I was nervous. My father had never taken me there before. Not to see my cousins. Not to see my Granda. Until then I'd never been further east than Buchanan Street. He parked up. He said we were going a walk to see his first home. Before he could roll the window up a wee bandit dressed as a joker tapped the bonnet and said –Geez a quid, al watch yer motor. Father picked through a rubber band roll of notes and said –Dinny joost watch it, wash it.

My father told the boy to get his wee pals, a sponge and fill a bucket with water and soap. For this they'd each get two bob. He said if their mammies complain –tell them Eh King wants his car cleaned.

We went to see the house. It was nothing special.

When we came back there were four boys standing neatly in a row, bucket and sponge in hand. The car was sparkling. He paid them, saying –Noo ahtz fur yer mammy n daddy. Then he produced a crisp five-pound note. –N ahtz fur yous. Spend it, save it – dae wut ye want wae it. Just dinny tell eny cunt where ye goat it. One wee boy looked up at me, said –wutsupwayhum? henotawkorsutin? I muttered –Only when I need to. The group shot me a look, then they took the cash and split.

When we got back in the car I noticed Father had left the keys in the ignition. As we drove off he told me:

–These are your people, son. You have to earn their respect.

My father ejects another dribble of faecal matter. I call the nurse.

My father always said he wanted to come back to Cumberland Street to die. Like a seagull going back to the ocean. I couldn't face sticking him in the housing with all the schemies, but the new builds are good enough. His address still says 474 Cumberland Street, but in truth his block is on Oregon Place. Those blocks have a terrible problem with damp, but they'll last another five years. Even if my father will not. As I walk down the close I am pleased by the smell of disinfectant.

I'm just about to unlock my Honda when I feel a familiar pain in my arse.

–Alright, Monty? How are you on this fine day?

–I am fine, Mr Smith.

–Never were much of a talker, were you? Shall I wait on your sister?

Morris Gallagher is far too cheeky to have ever been a great journalist. He was, at one time, a good one. He tried to write a story on me back in the nineties, when I was running Phast Travel. We sold cheap package holidays – but, as is often the case with cheap, we had issues with overbooked flights. Add that on to the tightening regulation of the time and some bad luck with mechanical failure… weather conditions and so on, I had to cancel around a thousand orders. No refunds.

Morris hounded me for a statement. Once he caught me going into my sister's close. I ran in. The door locked behind me. I hid in my sister's bedroom. He buzzed and buzzed and buzzed. Eventually I broke and answered it. But I put on a stupid high-pitched voice and said –Monty's just left, sorry!

This sarky cunt likes to bring it up. He thinks it unsettles me.

Does it fuck.

–My sister is trying to care for my seriously ill father. I would appreciate it if you did not bother her.

–No worries, big man, I'm not interested in your dad. What's the score with the Merchant Titty?

–I thought you said that name was 'trivialising tabloid trollop'?

–Any word on your meeting with the council today?

–It's at two o'clock.

–Monty – just read out your press release so I can write it down and fuck off.

–The red light district in the Merchant City has brought considerable regeneration to an entire section of Glasgow City Centre. By working in partnership with Glasgow City Council, Police Scotland and Social Services we have managed to increase the safety and wellbeing of sex workers in this city. The trial period has shown that the sex industry can be a force for social good, as well as an attractive touristic asset. We look forward to continuing this close relationship with the Council, Police Sco—

–Aye aye: the wanks, the filth, the social and the scum all in bed with each other got it.

–Next time just ask my secretary to email you the release.

–But then I wouldn't get to look you in the eye as you reel it off. You're getting better at it, Monty! Catch ye. Try not to shag any dogs on the way to your meeting.

–Grand hope you manage to fuck your fat wife with your Argos pen dick tonight you fucking arse.

He shoots me that look and gets in his Mercedes.

He thinks he got one over me. The bastard. I give my steering wheel a slap. Fuck's sake, Montgomery. Fuck's sake. As I sit staring at the logo surrounded by the plush, soft leather on the wheel my iPhone buzzes.

–Hullo hullo!

–What do you want?

–Z'at eny wey ae treat an auld pawl?

–What do you want?

–Didny stey lang it yer da'z, didje? Coodny huv bin mair'n hawf an oor.

–What do you want?

–Shockingsoitis. Wey eh auld gaffer'z gittin treateid.

–I am going to hang up now.

–Hawl hawl hawl. Joost wanteid tay ask how oor boys didny get intae – wuts it ye cry aht dancin agaen? Eh wan fulla poofs?

–G.O.L.F.

–Aye, so ye fuckin know ey didny make it in en.

–Yes.

–Must huv bin a mistaek, eh, Wee Monty Fuck? No tay worry but. Cuttla guyz'll be roon yer wanky piece shoap tae make up eh losseez. Two a'cloack awreet fur ye? Shud only need aboot hunnard tun ae keep ays sweet.

–Is that all you wanted to say?

–Iz aht aw? IZ AHT AW? LISTEN HERE, YA SNIDEY STUCK-UP—

I hang up. G.O.L.F is the crown jewel in my empire. When all the old men were pouring their efforts into the smack trade, I was expanding into a completely untapped market. The Pink Pound. That's what they used to call it. Glasgow thinks of itself as a rough city. For a populace that bears as many slashes as it does – they do like to tell you about how it's the knife crime capital of Europe. Or rather – how it was the knife crime capital of Europe. Glasgow doesn't want anyone to tarnish its hard-man reputation. But I do what all the others won't. So I opened up a few gay-friendly cafes, a pub here and there. When the time was right I bought the old shipyard storage units in the Merchant City and made them into Scotland biggest queer-friendly late licence venue. I will not have anyone encroach on my territory.

But I've got a plan. And just the woman to carry it out. As I drive to Peace I fire off a few texts.

–Hello Zara. Have you any appointments with Mr Donnelly today?

–No at the mo xx.

–I want you to phone him and make an appointment for as soon as possible. After you've finished, tell him my father has died.

–Aw, sorry bbz it doesn't work like that. Clients come to me xx.

–I know how it works. Make it work.

–Will it be worth my while? ;) xox.

–A thousand times over.

–Anything you say bossman xxxx.

I met Zara when I had that trouble down at Shoogle. She was a PR lassy and occasional gl(ass) collector. Shoogle was my first venture into straight boy clubbing. The place was designed from the ground up to stimulate a state of panic. Booming speakers with the treble set too high, erratically flashing lights and staffed exclusively by beautiful women. The plan was to put the men in the highest possible state of anxiety – then sell them the solution: alcohol! The only problem was since most of the fit girls were on the payroll none of the boys were getting their hole. This meant we had a couple of fights every night. Because straight people are animals. What the boys wanted was a bit of power over their peers. So I thought we could reduce violence if we installed a two-way mirror in the girls' toilets. Give the boys a chance to get one back on the frigid sluts, maybe have a wank and go home. Nobody gets hurt, everyone has a good time – I make lots of money. Perfect. The only problem was this generation doesn't know how to keep its fucking mouth shut. The story ended up breaking because some idiot put a photo on Instagram. It was of himself in the booth watching Zara wash her hands while he flexed for the camera. When Zara found out she didn't go to the press. She didn't go to the cops. She came to me. She told me if I cooked the books so it looked like she had been bar manager there for three years she'd solve it. Christ knows how she did, but one week after the story broke Shoogle was back open for business.

She's been working in the windows down the Merchant Titty for the last six months. Honestly, I would have given her an operational position if she wanted it. But she understands the importance of learning a business from the ground up.

My first job was scrubbing dishes in one of my father's money-laundering rackets. At that job I learned something very important about the leisure industry. Hire frustrated artists. For, you see, a chef is a frustrated artist. They are tuned into their senses – smell, taste, sight etc. Philosophers of aesthetics, really. Because of the passion that being switched on to your surroundings inspires – they will work at something they love for seventy hours a week. Even if you only pay them for thirty-five. Accounting for the fifty-six hours they should spend in bed, that leaves forty-two for their spare time. That is six hours a day. Or two days in a row – if they can steal a few hours from sleep. For a man in the leisure industry, this is both the perfect worker and the perfect customer. Give them a small discount in your pubs, clubs and eateries and they will bring all their friends until they all drink themselves to death.

The meeting is a formality, really. I'll admit, there is a small thrill that comes from being in those smoky rooms where dirty dealings get made. But it's always so much better in your imagination. In my mind: I'm going to be waved through by suited security agents, led into a back room off a councillor's office where we'll smoke cigars and toast fine wines to printing a big fat pile of money we don't even fuckin' need anyway, then we'll tear up a plan to redevelop abandoned land into a community centre in Possil and replace it with a youthy sponsored by Mad Dog 20/20, then we'll wipe our arses with letters complaining about compulsory purchase orders in East-End for the Chris Hoy velodrome, all while wearing gold medallions and freaky orange wizard robes.

But actually you just go into a room with a guy called Tim, a dyke called Joan, a bimbo Tim wants to put his prick in and an empty chair where the real boss would be if he wasn't reading Heat online and nursing a semi in his office. You read press releases at each other. You say buzzwords like tourism and regeneration. You sign a piece of paper. You leave.

As the kids say: patch that.

I send that wee piece Charlie a text telling him to go to the meeting for me. He's competent. I hired him to network within the gay club scene for me – I kept him around because he's a hotty. That boy knows how to read a press release and literally nothing else.

I park up outside Peace. I want to sit on the patio seats for when Donnelly's boys turn up. My skin is tinged with just enough yellow at the wrong end of summer to look sickly. People instinctively look away from me. I am the grey blur. But there is still no sense in taking unnecessary risks. Oh, Mr Donnelly – I did have a commitment at two o'clock, but I've moved some things around just for you.

I have a bit of time to kill before Donnelly's boys turn up. I take out my burner phone and compose sexually threatening messages to contacts from my business phone.

I'm halfway through writing a text to Morris telling him that he should lube his arsehole and his entire family's arseholes because tonight am gonny – when the main event arrives.

A white van pulls up. Two men get out.

The first is Shovel Hans. He's a German. Defected from East Berlin in 1986 by digging under the Berlin Wall with his bare hands when he was just two years old. He still only speaks Russian in a thick Hebridean accent. He told me once that Donald Trump is a double agent programmed by the KGB to be a satire of American values, created to serve as a villain in propaganda reels. However, the programming was suspended partway through – due to a soviet ethics committee decision – and so they dumped him into the Gulf of Mexico. There he met a powerful bridge troll, who said he could make him into a real boy if only Trump sucked him off. Once Trump had successfully swallowed the rancid ejaculate, the bridge troll cast a spell which created a parallel reality (which we exist in) where Trump could come about as a result of natural processes. That is why, Shovel Hans often remarks, you cannot trust bridge trolls. They would rather bend reality than confront it.

Shovel Hans is completely off his nut.

The second thug is Tam the Bike. Named so because he stabbed someone. While riding a bike.

The pair run into my cafe. Shovel Hans grabs a man by the arm and puts him out on his arse. The other punters follow suit. Six walk out. At an average spend of £6.58 for six customers they have already cost me £39.48. I can't hear them – but I imagine Tam the Bike is probably shouting some uninspired diatribe about how any cunt that grasses is fuckin deed, errz tha sayf big maan! CUMBIE FUCKIN RULE etc. etc. Shovel Hans is putting the real work in here. Calm. Collected. Dangerous. My staff look scared. But they're following their training.

See: the thing about Peace is that in our cafés we care about the future. We care about leaving behind a sustainable environment for our children. That's why we don't print receipts, don't give out straws and don't accept paper or metal currency. You pay using an app on your phone.

We don't keep any fucking money onsite, you absolute pair of wallopers!

It dawns on Shovel Hans first. He leaves immediately. Tam, on the other hand, is obviously frustrated that the mission was a bust. He takes a chair and tries to smash a window, but it bounces and falls to the floor. The glass is chipped. Easy fix, though: one hour's labour and parts. Fifty pound.

Still. £89.48 is not quite ten grand, is it?

Autoglass beware: I'll autoglass your face.

My iPhone buzzes.

–Eh… hullo, Mr King.

–What do you want?

–Av joost… ah… heard aboot yer old man. Am sorry, Monty.

–What do you want?

–Just to let ye know err's nay bad blood here. You're eh king noo.

I hang up.

I send a text to Morris asking him to meet me at the concierge desk at the Caley Road high rises in an hour.

I love this city. I love the people. I love the grid the streets make. I love the green copper. Like this city is a circuit board. All it needs is a jolt. I have a vision for it. I want Glasgow to be said in the same breath as Paris, Berlin or Rome. They say Edinburgh is the Athens of the north. Fuck Athens. Their empire lasted a fraction of a moment. It is a shame that Glaswegians have such a wonderful spark about them. A spark only bright enough to burn out.

Glasgow was built to be a part of history – it was not built for them. The history of this city is a history of its inhabitants trying to own it – but the truth is Glasgow owns them. And when their time comes it will disown them. And in a generation their lineage will be nothing but teuchters.

I park up outside my father's flat. I leave my keys in the ignition.

I let myself into the house. I find my father sound asleep in his bed, with a half-eaten sandwich next to him. I take the pillow his head is resting on. For a moment – I think he is going to wake up. His eyes open. He gives me a look. I hold it. There is no flash of recognition. No understanding. He knows something bad is about to happen. His body tenses. I push the pillow into his face. His arms struggle weakly. He puts his sallow hand on my wrist. I push harder. His fingers go limp but his body keeps jerking.

It's pathetic. The way animals cling to life. I remember seeing a pigeon with a broken wing struggling on Byres Road once. A sweet young woman wanted to call the RSPCA. I walked to it and I stamped on it. The pigeon kept struggling. I stamped on it again. Still it beat its twisted wings. I picked it up, I snapped its neck and I put it in the bin.

There is a story that does the rounds about my father. Once upon a time a smackhead wouldn't pay his tic. Not an uncommon practice. My father was normally happy to let the street-level dealers take care of it. But this poor fool made the mistake of running his mouth in one of my father's pubs. So my father went to his house, alone, to have a little chat. When the junky continued to disrespect him, my father took a nail gun and crucified him to the floor. Two eleven-inch nails straight through his wrists. One through his feet. And one in his gut. Then my father dragged the junky's daughter out of bed and raped her as the junky begged not to be killed.

That version of the story is bullshit. My father never went alone.

I was holding his tool box.

High rises were built to prepare children for prison. The door being controlled by a man in a white shirt subtly implants the notion that you are allowed to leave only on a faceless state agent's say-so. The bedrooms are little better than cells. The building is designed for efficiency – not living. Cladding isn't going to change that. Morris signals the concierge, and the glass doors slide open. He spots me. He says something snide – but I don't listen. I motion for him to follow me. We get in the lift and I take him to the top floor. His lips move. But he isn't saying a thing. I take him out to the washing line, and we look out over the New Gorbals.

–Would you have ever thought there'd be houses like those in the Gorbals?

–It's a natural progression. It is relatively close to the city centre. It was cheap: for food, rent, council tax. Once the area was deindustrialised it stopped being so dirty and smelly. Thus there was no reason for it to be so cheap. Students and artists move here trying to piss off mummy and daddy. Professionals move there because it's trendy. Then they either civilise or push out the locals.

–Civilise? Monty. You are such a wank.

–That's what empires do, Morris.

–Wank?

–We civilise. We build statues. Make rules. Then we make it a rule that you have to speak our language if you want to build statues. You know what else we do?

–What?

–We make lots and lots of money. Do you read history, Morris?

–Yes.

–Then I am sure you are aware of Glasgow's position as one the largest slave-ports in the UK and Europe. It was not shipwrighting that built this city – it was in fact millions upon millions of black bodies crammed into impossibly vast boats. Some see this as a black mark against us. I do not. The truth is – at one point slavery was the most efficient technology for producing capital. If most of the work is picking, digging, hoeing etc. then it only requires an obedient mind and strong body. If a small section of the population are enslaved then it leaves a surplus of time and energy. This is used to create things like roads, train tracks – infrastructure. This requires more planning and planners to plan it. But it also requires better-trained workers to do it. Once the infrastructure is built then there is even more surplus time and energy! And so society develops until the majority of the work requires high levels of training. Even the easiest jobs require literacy and numeracy these days. This means slavery as a technology has become obsolete.

In order to learn you need three things: the surplus time/energy to do it, an environment of quiet contemplation/security to do it in – and the proper motivation. If a slave even has half a chance at any of these things – they will quickly free themselves. So our workers cannot be slaves. And since they are now citizens they have the same right as everyone else to shape our culture. We assimilate them. We apologise for their rough start, but – always add the but – by speaking our language they are admitting their forebears were savages. So why, at Glasgow Uni, are there countless descendants of slavers crying out for streets they've never lived on to be renamed? Guilt.

Look out at the Gorbals. Do you think it was better back in the day? When my father and his lot robbed, beat, cut and stabbed their way into high society? Was it better when junkies slept on every park bench? Or is it better now we've ripped out the benches? My father tried to make a Glasgow for hard men when what we needed was a Glasgow for sweet women. That is what the Merchant Titty is all about. I am giving the young women of this city a chance to rise high using their native language. The language of their bodies. It is prostitution as an economic technology. They will lie in the beds of powerful men. They will watch. They will learn. And our next generation of women will not be slaves. Should I feel guilty?

–I hope you know why people hate you.

–I do. I am not easily categorised. I am neither one of us nor one of them. An innovator. An outsider.

–You talk shite. Constant and total shite.

I flash him a look.

–I called you up here because I wanted to give you a parting gift.

–Spit it out.

–My father has died.

I let the silence hang.

–He choked to death on a sandwich due to complications related to Alzheimer's. I am greatly saddened and would ask that any questions relating to his life be directed to my sister, Mary King, as she is the family historian. He will be missed.

–I will never contact you ever again if you can say one genuine, heartfelt reason you will miss your father.

–Just one?

–Just one.

-Never again?

-Never again.

–He loved me.

I briefly think about pushing Morris through the window. He leaves by the close. I let him walk ahead, taking a moment to savour the view. As I look over my father's empire and the new lands I have conquered – I see a wee boy break my window, get in my car and drive it away.

21. ZARA SCROLLS ENDLESSLY THROUGH FACEBOOK

Zara Chisolm
Just now · ⊙ ▾

Congratulations to **@Jodie Whittaker** on her appointment as the New Dr Who. Rock it hon **xoxo** 🍸🍸😄

Sebastian Weasel Haven't watched it in years (mostly because of that bloody Moffat haha) but this here has pricked my ears
Will deffo swatch it when she premiers.
Like · Reply · Just now

Addy Zgame I don't watch Dr Who
Cos it's fucking shite.
They don't show it in pubs and
that's where I am on monday nights
But him being a woman?
That lark is retarded
If he's a woman
how's he gonna park the tardis?
Like · Reply · Just now

Sebastian Weasel I take it you believe
Dr Who has to be a man
But have you even been to uni?
I have so I can say confidently,
Pal... it's the 21st Century...
Like · Reply · Just now

Addy Zgame Not saying Time Lords can't be ladies too
Just saying if you're gonna change the bits for tits
you should change the title too.
How about Nurse Who? 😄😂
Like · Reply · Just now

Sebastian Weasel I cannot understand these sexist attitudes!
How can someone with a mum
and maybe even a sister too
Denigrate the position of women
Spewing hate to masturbate
It's so ego driven.
Like · Reply · Just now

Save post

Edit Post

Change Date

Embed

Turn off notifications for this post

Show in tab

Hide from Timeline

Delete

Remove Text Effects

Turn off translations

 Addy Zgame Fuck up tight jean cunt.
Like · Reply · Just now

 Sebastian Weasel Abuse! The last refuge
Of the man with no argument.
Like · Reply · Just now

 Addy Zgame I'll abuse your face.
Like · Reply · Just now

 Sebastian Weasel Take your toxic masculinity elsewhere.
Like · Reply · Just now

 Addy Zgame Cuck
Like · Reply · Just now

Sebastian Weasel (2)   21:36
I'm so sorry you have to put up with such Silly wee boys. ...

Addy Zgame (1)   21:34
Hey girl, can't believe the fannies That are sniffing aroon y...

Zara Chisolm   + ■ 📞 ⚙ ✕

Thanks sweety xx, I'm out in
Edinburgh tonight
But I'll give you a message
when I get back 🙂 xox

           m   + ■ 📞 ⚙ ✕

                                              21:09

Hey girl, can't believe the
fannies
That are sniffing aroon ye
 fancy a night on the toon?   I'm so sorry you have to put
I feel like howling at the   up with such
moon.   Silly wee boys. It must be
                                     hard to raise your voice
                                     But don't worry honey- obvs
                                     like I'm there
                                     If you need to give these
                                     troglodytes a scare.
                                     Or just shoulder on which to
                                     dry away your cares x

✏ **Status**   📷 **Photo/Video**   📹 **Live video**   🚩 **Life Event**

   FUCK IT

Never walk in another man's shoes.

Walk in your own.

They're the only ones you have.

But walk down the same path sometimes. See what they see

& think your own thoughts.

Everything you do will come back to you.

A sudden hush comes around my room
As the wind outside whistles like a teapot
And my MacBook glows blue,
Then up comes a sudden torrent rush,
Pulls me tongue-first through
The fibre optic wires.
Oh bugger. Oh bugger.
Oh bug
g

My fuckin speakers are on the blink.

                                        g

Phones spazzing out 'n' aw.

                              g

Fuck's sake. Fuck's sake

            fuuu   ggggg
        uuuuuu   ggggggggg
        uu   uu   uu   gggg   g   gg
            ggg   uu   uu
                    UU   GG
                    ggg
er   g   gggg   UCK'S SAKE!

I wake up in an alien place.
Outside there isn't a single white face.
I can't make out what language they are talking.
I could be anywhere but Scotland!
I do what I always do when I first wake up.
Check my laptop.

                              Aw fuck.
                    I dunno what the fuck
                        Is going on but
                    I'm in fuckin Finnieston.
                    That's fuckin two busses.

74

Fuck's sake.
Where's my phone?

I am Addy Zgame.
That isn't a name.

I check my phone that's just got upgraded two gens
Nice-looking flash camera lens.
Lift up my shirt to take a wee phoaty
But some cunt's bumped my boady!

It's that prick from Facebook.

It's that prick from Facebook

...   ...
...   ...
...   ...

bet he watches fucked-up porn.
bet he watches fucked-up porn.
Cuckold Made To Clean Creampie And Bulls Cock - Pornhub.com

Facial Abuse Compilation Porn Videos | Pornhub.com

Knew it.

Knew it.

Click back to his Facebook chats.
He's got four unread messages
From girls that to me never talk back.
And he's sliding into Zara's DMs.

Well – if there's one thing I know,
It's that no woman has ever wanted
An unsolicited photo of male genitalia.

This bitch is chatting shit
About me to Zara THE princess!
If I see him in G-hill,
Swear to god I'm gonny kill.

Hell – might as well
Squash the competition's chances
While I'm stuck in
This skinny bastard cell.

 **Addy Zgame**
Addy sent a photo.

21:07

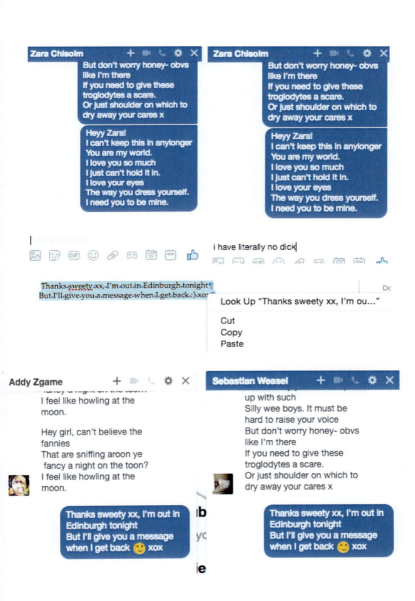

Zara Chisolm + ▣ ☎ ✿ ✕

But don't worry honey- obvs
like I'm there
If you need to give these
troglodytes a scare.
Or just shoulder on which to
dry away your cares x

Heyy Zara!
I can't keep this in anylonger
You are my world.
I love you so much
I just can't hold it in.
I love your eyes
The way you dress yourself.
I need you to be mine.

🖼 🙂 (GIF) ☺ 📎 🎮 📷 🗐 👍

Thanks sweety xx, I'm out in Edinburgh tonight¶
But I'll give you a message when I get back :) xox

Zara Chisolm + ▣ ☎ ✿ ✕

But don't worry honey- obvs
like I'm there
If you need to give these
troglodytes a scare.
Or just shoulder on which to
dry away your cares x

Heyy Zara!
I can't keep this in anylonger
You are my world.
I love you so much
I just can't hold it in.
I love your eyes
The way you dress yourself.
I need you to be mine.

i have literally no dick

🖼 🙂 (GIF) ☺ 📎 🎮 📷 🗐 👍

Dc

Look Up "Thanks sweety xx, I'm ou..."

Cut
Copy
Paste

Addy Zgame + ▣ ☎ ✿ ✕

fancy a night on the toon?
I feel like howling at the
moon.

Hey girl, can't believe the
fannies
That are sniffing aroon ye
fancy a night on the toon?
I feel like howling at the
moon.

Thanks sweety xx, I'm out in
Edinburgh tonight
But I'll give you a message
when I get back 🙂 xox

lb

yc

ie

Sebastian Weasel + ▣ ☎ ✿ ✕

up with such
Silly wee boys. It must be
hard to raise your voice
But don't worry honey- obvs
like I'm there
If you need to give these
troglodytes a scare.
Or just shoulder on which to
dry away your cares x

Thanks sweety xx, I'm out in
Edinburgh tonight
But I'll give you a message
when I get back 🙂 xox

But he sent a picture of his dick!
Girls do not want pictures of dicks.
Girls want romance, to be cherished.
Girls want someone to hold them,
Protect them, support them.
She must be so fucking dumb
If she's into this stupid cunt.
I don't even know why I bother talking to her!
She's always out in fucking Edinburgh.

But he's talking like a total gimp.
Girls do not want beta orbiters.
They want men that make the first move,
That do their best to impress,
Pop a little flex, keep flash with cash.
Girls want alphas.
And she's got some cheek 'cause
That's what she sent me last week.

22. ZARA IS IPARA

```
DO NOT BE PARANOID
D                     D
O         T           O
N         A           N
O         K           O
T         E           T
B         L           B
E         I           E
P         N           P
A         E           A
R         H           R
A         E           A
N         R           N
O         E           O
I         O           I
D                     D
DO NOT BE PARANOID
```

23. ZARA TAKES A PHONE CALL FROM HER MOTHER ABOUT SARAH

I caught my reflection in a puddle.
So I stopped going outside after it rained.

I caught my reflection staring at my dirty pants.
So I washed them.

I caught my reflection sneering at my shoulders.
So I went back to sleep.

Then my reflection caught me,
Asked if my childhood was happy.

I told it yes so it wouldn't cry.

I caught my reflection playing my piano.
It wasn't very good, so I let it practise instead of me.

I caught my reflection planning an endless day.
So I didn't sleep and got on with it.

I caught my reflection in a wing mirror.
So I stopped walking on streets with parked cars.

Then my reflection caught me,
Said I looked too much like my daddy,

So I saved up to have his ears pinned back.

I caught my reflection in my phone screen.
So I never turned it off and kept it locked on a selfie.

I caught my reflection in the bathroom mirror.
So I took it down.

I caught my reflection in the bedroom closet mirror.
So I took a sheet and pinned it up.

But he woke up.

He tore the sheet down.

He screamed at my reflection.

He told it that we didn't want it here.

He told it it had spent my whole life lying to me.

He begged it please please please just fuck off.

Then he sat down in a pile of his dirty clothes.
Lit a joint.
And fell asleep.

I picked up what I could to put it in the washing machine
(where I caught my reflection),

Cleaned last night's dishes in the sink
(where I caught my reflection)

And cooked him his breakfast.

24. STALKER

On the first day, trees feast when
their seeds split and shoot.
Tomorrow, they'll set down roots.
On Sunday, they scrap for sunlight
and finally grasp it.

We are an untroubling blur that
passes by. Whole generations
coming and going in one weekend.

When we cut them down they are
gone in a thousandth of a moment.

I take the knife and carve our initials
into the tree.

You never left the house that day.

PART 3:

WEED

25. ZARA WAKES UP AND TRIES TO HAVE A WANK

The Illustrious Career of Sarah Chisolm MA Bates

Channel 900

I was staying over at my cousin's.
We'd spent all night drinking Irn-Bru 32,
Chatting up boys on MSN
And eating slabs of chocolate.
My cousin had got her period.
I still hadn't yet.

When there were no more episodes of South Park on,
My cousin took the remote
And flipped it over to channel 900.
We called in to bam up the hoors.

But when my cousin fell asleep
I flipped it back over.
I saw the women dance, phone in hand,
And I thought how sweet it would be
To have a cock.

Cherry Staar, I will never forget you.
I owe my first wank and all others to you.

1st High Score: 4

They told us to say NO if we didn't want to have sex.

Mr Merrel taught us about condoms.
He had a cute, squeaky English voice.
When he took the banana out,
I thought about slipping my hand over his cock.

At lunch I went to the girls' toilets
In the CDT corridor.

I lay on my front on the floor,
Hand jammed through a loosened belt
And buttoned-up skinny jeans.
Pants constricting
As I twitch and spin.

They never taught us to say yes when we wanted it.
I learned that on my own.

Danger Wank

A danger wank is when you shout on your mum before you cum.
For beginners it's best to do it at the point of no returning.
But Grant Garrick's record was when he was two thirds in.

Fucking. Pussies.

Mam and her new boyfriend were taking us to France.
They decided to drive there so they could explore better.
But driving from Inverness to Normandy
Takes forty-two hours of non-stop sitting.

Mam was asleep.
My brother was asleep.

Mam's boyfriend was driving
In the dead of night.

I came twice.
Deadpan face.
The subtlest movements
Under my underwear.

I think I got away with it.
But just before I really fell asleep,
I heard my mam's boyfriend
Roll the window down.

2nd High Score: 7

We were on a Geography trip up Mount Fyrish.
I had this big jumper on, went past my knees,
Over a loose pair of waterproof trackies.
I wrapped my arms round body, dangling sleeves,

Walking is boring.
The teacher is boring
Geography is boring.
My classmates are boring.
The Highlands are boring.

Wanking is not!

Mutual Masturbation

Bathed in blue light.
You like?
You are mine.

Our eyes feast.

Your screen name was
Everybody likes a joke but no one loves a fool.
So I said –I love you. As a joke. –cus you're a fool :)
But then you said –I love you too.

You pointed the camera at your cock
But what really got me off
Was watching you run your fingers through your hair,

Arms tensed, flexing what cute muscle was there.

Puppy love is the strongest kind of love.
It consumes every ounce of your soul,
Every grain of your pain
And every part of your whole.

Score Void Due to Use of Performance-Enhancing Drugs

If you have never experienced the pure joy

Of smoking grass and having a wank,

Stop what you are doing right now.

Look up https://www.pornhub.com/view_video.
php?viewkey=ph5608b3b2d5745

Suck a bucket.

Breathe deeply, deeply.

I got my all-time high score the first day I tried it.

RETARDED PENIS

He says he really really wants to.
His cock is hard. The tip is wet.
The condom fits. The mood was set.

He says he wants to give me everything.
Every ounce of his soul.
Every grain of his pain.
Every part of his whole.

But he just can't penetrate.

Fucking liar.

I lie next to him, swishing my clit
Back and forth and up and down,
A mood swing on a roundabout.

He thinks I just want to fuck.
I want love.
Show me love.

The First Wank After a Break-Up

The time I was wearing that black and white dress.
The time I sang a song for you.
The time you took me dancing and looked at me like I was the
only girl in the world.
The time we kissed on the kerb outside the café.
The time you laid me on the bed and told me you loved me.
The first time we used a mirror when I looked so good.
The time you said I acted all sweet and cute but deep down I
was a dirty whore who needed cock.
All the times you ran your fingers softly along my back.
The time you washed me with lotion, stroked me in the bath.
The time you swung me around and around and around.

I left all our best memories soaking in my bedsheets.

Three-Year Marathon

High scores are all well and good,
But the greatest achievement of a true master
'bater is the marathon.

Once every twenty-four hours is easy enough.
Just one when you wake up.
The once every twelve hours
Adds a bit of commitment,

One on waking, one before sleeping,
But once every six hours:
That. Is a challenge.

The method is:
1) Sleep for two hours at a time.
2) Eat microwave food
Only when you get so hungry
You remember to.
3) Watch pornography which features
Your darkest desires.

26. ZARA THINKS ABOUT UPDATING HER C.V.

ZARA CHISOLM

07572 217 064
sarahchisolmis@hotmail.co.uk

19 Annette Street
Govanhill
Glasgow
G42 8LJ

Profile
Glezga Girl.

Experience
Window Artist — 2017 - Present
The only job I have ever loved.

Glass Collector — 2015 - 2017
Picked up glasses. Was hired so the bar manager could eye fuck me, customers could molest me and wanky students could be intimidated by me. It was the same 10 minutes repeated over and over and over and over and over and over and

Sweet Fuck All — 2012 - 2015
Smoked hash all day every day to get over my 'disability' lol free money aff the government GIRUY.

Pizza Slice — 2011 - 2012
Handed out flyers for NJ Slice dressed as a giant pizza on Sauchiehall street from midnight till 4am. Learnt what it meant to be dehumanised and objectified in exchange for great benefits and a low effort job.

Education
Left school at 16. N whit?

Skills
Can do 10 keepy-ups in a row with a flat ball. .

References
your da 0141 xxx xxxx

HH

27. STALKER

I don't want to be here. But I cannot leave. I can feel slack strings pulling at my hands and feet. You left to go to the Co-op. Finally. You left the door unlocked. I let myself into your hovel. The smell of cat pish hits me like a thrown shoe. My eyes water. My throat gags. I tip-toe around your bungalow. Like a ballerina dancing on egg shells. The floor is littered with spilt ash trays and empty bottles of gut-rot cider. Your rancid arse gas has mixed with the fug of the cat shit. It lies around like evidence. The first clue was the piled-up letters. The second clue was the mattress on the floor. It was crawling with cockroaches. I sit on it. From here I can see through the window. I can see the tree I have been sitting under for the last two weeks. In the toilet there is a bucket wedged under a burst pipe. Pishy, shitey water drip drip splats. It's near overflowing. When you come home I am sat in your cupboard. The strings on my hands tighten. I rub the blunt edge of the blade.

28. SARAH'S EX COMES TO HER HOUSE UNINVITED

I came in drunk last night.
Had an itch I want to scratch
On my triggered finger,
So I grabbed my lass and gave her that whisper,

But when I couldn't cum,
I took my fist and I
pressed it into her.

I don't think it hurt her.
But it's the threat that's the issue here.

I went to the rape crisis centre.
They said they don't let men enter.
I said –HOW THE FUCK NOT?
…

–Because of that.

See, the women in here have been attacked.
We can't expose them to all of that.
Plus we're only trained to deal with the certain way
That women react. We can't help you here.

So I wrote fuck up
On the side of a dump truck,
Then I stole it and drove it
Back to the slums
To celebrate my good luck!

Back at the flat I found a pound pizza in the freezer.
Can't eat it 'cause I can't heat it, so I discreetly leave it
To defrost, then rot. MY CAT!
Says I'm as cold as Jack Frost.
So I froze a bottle of Frosty's, ate the ice
And lost my heed. I said to the cat,
–FUCK JACK FROST!

I'll stick the claw end of a hammer in his nostril, pull it
TIGHT LIKE
I'm ripping anal beads out your dad's
SHITE PIPE!

Whoa.

Just caught myself in the mirror there.
Almost did not recognise myself for a minute there,
I've lost a lot of weight and lost a lot of hair,
And I'm stronger and taller,
Now you can see the scar by my eye
And the devil's mark under my ear,
I can see why I might give some people the fear.

But I still feel like a collar-chewing wee boy
Who needs to shout and scream to get heard above the noise,

Because no one ever listens to me,
Unless I'm pretending I'm happy,
Or they're full of mandy,
Or there's something they could get off me,

Only massage my back so
I'll massage their ego.

–I see you like my little brother.

Went on my phone to escape,
But all my mates were talking
About rape rates
In the United States.

When I looked up,
I was in a pub.
I thought – GREAT!

But I realised
It was a poetry night.

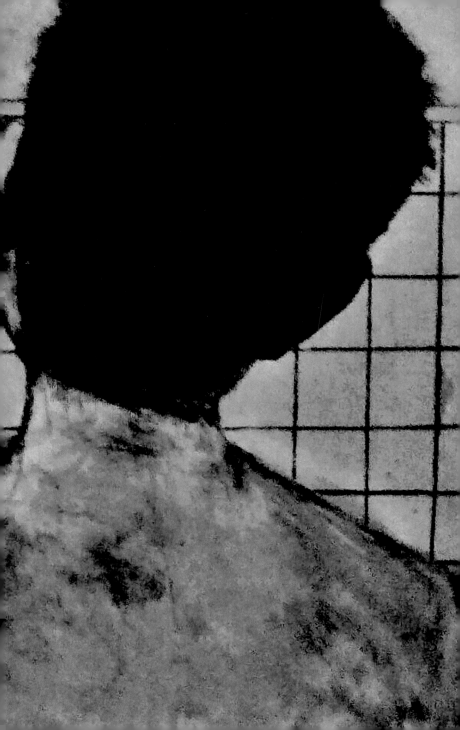

I thought – shite.

Then a collar-chewer took the mic
To apologise for all the mistakes men make,
Like war. Genocide. And rape.

After that it was all
Bitches bitching about being bitches,
Until one bitch with the bad case
Of resting bitch face,
Coke nose and ketamine spoon
Got wired to the fucking moon,
And decided to share with the room
Her open wounds.

–She was boozy, but she was wooozzzy too.

Bedroom eyes and a cracking dress,
The husky voice leaves me a mess,
She's on stage, she's got to impress,
Commanding attention is a way
Of taking back the power, I guess,

BUT ALL MY MIND IS GOING TO IS SEX!

Access your feelings:

I feel frustrated I could not achieve orgasm last night.
I feel under a great deal of pressure to enjoy sex.
I feel jealous of the attention that women get.

Then I met a radfem.
She said I was one of them awful men.
So I says –Hen, you're a perfect ten!
Stick with me, I'll show you your best ever weekend.

Sinking rums and bedding ones,
Chewing blues and grooving twos,
Ketamine keys and kissing threes,

Smoking scores and scoring fours,
Saving lives and pulling fives,
Banging mixes and banging sixes,
Manna from heaven
When I winch a seven.
Paying mates' rates tay
Fornicate way eights,
Sniffing lines and shagging nines,
Sipping glens and nipping tens.

DRINKING MAD DOG AND
PUMPING YOUR MAW.
DRINKING MAD DOG AND
PUMPING YOUR MAW.

She said I was being abusive.
I said –You know FUCK-ALL about abuse.
Then some ginger cunt with four chins said to me:
–What's the problem, baby – get triggered, maybe?

NO! NO! I AM FINE. I AM FINE.
AM JUST RAGIN BECAUSE…
THESE POEMS ARE SO SHITE.

ABUSE DOESN'T RHYME.
ABUSE HAS NO METRE.
ABUSE IS NOT A METAPHOR.

ABUSE IS A COLLAR-CHEWING WEE BOY.
ABUSE IS WALKING TO ITS GRANNY
ABUSE CUT OVER THE BLACK BRIDGE.

ABUSE IS A LONER STALKING AROUND THE PARK.
ABUSE IS WALKING THROUGH THE PARK.

ABUSE THREW SHOES BEHIND A SKIP.
ABUSE TUGGED DOWN VICTIM'S PANTS.

ABUSE IS THE FINGERARSE.
ABUSE IS THE COCKMOUTH.

ABUSE IS THE SHITEPANTS.

ABUSE IS RUNNING AWAY.
ABUSE IS LAUGHING.
ABUSE CAN'T STOP LAUGHING.

ABUSE IS THE SHITE DRIPPING DOWN MY LEGS.

ABUSE IS FINDING ME.
ABUSE IS ASKING ME NOT TO TELL GRANNY.
ABUSE IS ME TELLING GRANNY.

ABUSE IS EATING UNTIL ITS BODY IS DISGUSTING.
ABUSE IS AFRAID OF TURNING INTO ITS CREATOR.
ABUSE CAN'T STOP CONSUMING HARDCORE
PORNOGRAPHY.
ABUSE CAN'T STOP SEEING PHANTOM FACES OF
RAPISTS.
ABUSE CAN'T STOP TWITCHING.

ABUSE IS PERPETRATOR.
ABUSE IS VICTIM.
ABUSE IS BYSTANDER.

She said –I don't think we should support men with a history
of abuse.

Then I realised the truth.

I am sorry.

Consider this my apology.

I've got to take responsibility,

Because the cycle brings it on itself.

But all I said was:

–You and everybody else.

29. ZARA LOOKS AT HER WATCH AND IT SAYS IT IS DEAL WITH YOUR SHIT O' CLOCK

12

11　　　JUST　　　1

10　　MOMENT　HAVING　2

A　　shit　　deal　　A

9　HAVING　AHH　MOMENT　3

JUST　your　with　JUST

8　　MOMENT　HAVING　4

7　　　　A　　　　5

6

30. ZARA EATS A HANDFUL OF TRAMADOL AND GETS THE MEGABUS FROM GLASGOW TO INVERNESS

In Glaschu a stately pleasure-dome I do decree:
Where Clyde, the sacred river, ran
Through sewers measureless to man,
   Down to a fishless sea.
So twice five miles of fertile ground
With walls and towers were girdled round;
And there were parks bright with flightless birds,
Where blossomed many a stunted tree;
And here were schemes ancient as the hills,
Enfolding sunny spots of the Green.

But oh! that deep romantic chasm which slanted
Down Finnieston athwart a railway arch cover!
A savage place! as holy and enchanted
As e'er beneath a waning moon was haunted
By woman wailing for her demon-lover!
From this chasm, ceaseless tunes were playing,
As if this earth in fast thick pants were exhaling,
A mighty memory momently was forced:
Amid whose swift half-intermitted burst
Huge fragments vaulted like rebounding hail,
Or bitter grain 'neath the credit card crush:
And 'mid these dancing rocks at once and ever
It flung up momently the sacred A9.
180 miles meandering with a mazy motion
Through hill and glen the sacred A9 ran,
Then reached the sewer measureless to man,
And sank in tumult to a lifeless ocean;
And 'mid this tumult Zara heard in her core
Ancestral voices prophesying war!
   The shadow of the dome of pleasure
   Cast midway on the Muir;
   Where was heard the mingled measure
   From the memory and the sewer.

It was a miracle of rare device,
A sunny pleasure-dome with foundations of shite!

   A lassy with a lyre
   In a vision once I saw:
   It was a fenian princess
   And on her lyre she plucked
   Strings of barbed wire,
   Singing 'Don't Be a Cunt' along.
   Could I revive within me
   Her symphony and song,
   To such a deep delight 'twould win me,

That with music loud and long,
I would build that dome in air,
That sunny dome! those foundations!
And all who heard should see them there,
And all should cry, Beware! Beware!
Her flashing eyes, her floating hair!
Weave a circle round her thrice,
And close your eyes with holy dread
For she on honey-dew hath fed,
And drunk the milk of Paradise.

31. ZARA SEES SARAH FOR THE FIRST TIME SINCE SHE LEFT MUIR OF ORD

Zara and Sarah grew the tree together.
Watered it with two litres of American Cola a day.
Smashed their window to let the light in.

But the house was full.

So Zara dug it up.
Replanted it in the woods
Among the wind and the moss.
Its true brothers.

–Do you remember when the mark was made?
Sarah asked Zara on a train, once. Zara muttered.
Sarah said she was just checking she wasn't going mental.
No need to speak of it again.

Zara stayed on that train.
But Sarah went back. Sarah
Dug the tree up. Planted it
Back in their old room.

The ceilings were too low.
But they said the trunk was too tall.

The sunlight it eats is filtered through fag smoke!
It only drinks water poisoned with corn syrup!
It grows, yes, but it only grows sideways!

Sarah winks at Zara.
Sarah points at the hole they broke to let the light in.
And Zara sees a branch bearing leaves
Poking out to the sun.

32. ZARA HAS A GOOD CRY

A Spell of Acceptance

Everything that happens

Happens because of your own actions
and agreeing to be the victim.

Take control.

33. STALKER

LOVE YOU I LOVE YOU I LOVE YOU I LOVE YOU I LOVE
YOU I LOVE YOU I LOVE YOU I LOVE YOU I LOVE YOU I
LOVE YOU I LOVE YOU I LOVE YOU I LOVE YOU I LOVE
YOU I LOVE YOU I LOVE YOU I LOVE YOU I LOVE YOU I
LOVE YOU I LOVE YOU I LOVE YOU I LOVE YOU I LOVE
YOU I LOVE YOU I LOVE YOU I LOVE YOU I LOVE YOU I
LOVE YOU I LOVE YOU I LOVE YOU I LOVE YOU I LOVE
YOU I LOVE YOU I LOVE YOU I LOVE YOU I LOVE YOU I
LOVE YOU I LOVE YOU I LOVE YOU I LOVE YOU I LOVE
YOU I LOVE YOU I LOVE YOU I LOVE YOU I LOVE YOU I
LOVE YOU I LOVE YOU I LOVE YOU I LOVE YOU I LOVE
YOU I LOVE YOU I LOVE YOU I LOVE YOU I LOVE YOU I
LOVE YOU I LOVE YOU I LOVE YOU I LOVE YOU I LOVE
YOU I LOVE YOU I LOVE YOU I LOVE YOU I LOVE YOU I
LOVE YOU I LOVE YOU I LOVE YOU I LOVE YOU I LOVE
YOU I LOVE YOU I LOVE YOU I LOVE YOU I LOVE YOU I
LOVE YOU I LOVE YOU I LOVE YOU I LOVE YOU I LOVE
YOU I LOVE YOU I LOVE YOU I LOVE YOU I LOVE YOU I
LOVE YOU I LOVE YOU I LOVE YOU I LOVE YOU I LOVE
YOU I LOVE YOU I LOVE YOU I LOVE YOU I LOVE YOU I
LOVE YOU I LOVE YOU I LOVE YOU I LOVE YOU I LOVE
YOU I LOVE YOU I LOVE YOU I LOVE YOU I LOVE YOU I
LOVE YOU I LOVE YOU I LOVE YOU I LOVE YOU I LOVE
YOU I LOVE YOU I LOVE YOU I LOVE YOU I LOVE YOU I
LOVE YOU I LOVE YOU I LOVE YOU I LOVE YOU I LOVE
YOU I LOVE YOU I LOVE YOU I LOVE YOU I LOVE YOU I
LOVE YOU I LOVE YOU I LOVE YOU I LOVE YOU I LOVE
YOU I LOVE YOU I LOVE YOU I LOVE YOU I LOVE YOU I
LOVE YOU I LOVE YOU I LOVE YOU I LOVE YOU I LOVE
YOU I LOVE YOU I LOVE YOU I LOVE YOU I LOVE YOU I
LOVE YOU I LOVE YOU I LOVE YOU I LOVE YOU I LOVE
YOU I LOVE YOU I LOVE YOU I LOVE YOU I LOVE YOU I
LOVE YOU I LOVE YOU I LOVE YOU I LOVE YOU I LOVE

DO NOT BE PARANOID

```
D                       D
O                       O
N       everyone        N
O       is looking at   O
T       you…            T
B                       B
E                       E
P                       P
A                       A
R                       R
A                       A
N                       N
O                       O
I           O           I
D                       D
```

DO NOT BE PARANOID

I like to watch people when they don't think they're being watched. Your eyes are different when you're alone. I think it must be the heat – or the smell – in here. Your eyes are melting. You drank two thirds of a 2l of white cider. You look like you're waiting for something. I wonder if you can still smell shite. Through the wooden slats on the cupboard door I see you look out the window. At our tree. If you scar a tree when it is young it will always bear a mark. But as it grows the mark will get smaller and smaller. In comparison. I think the tree will always feel it. I hope the tree will always feel it.

```
        j
            u
            s
                t
            h
    a
```

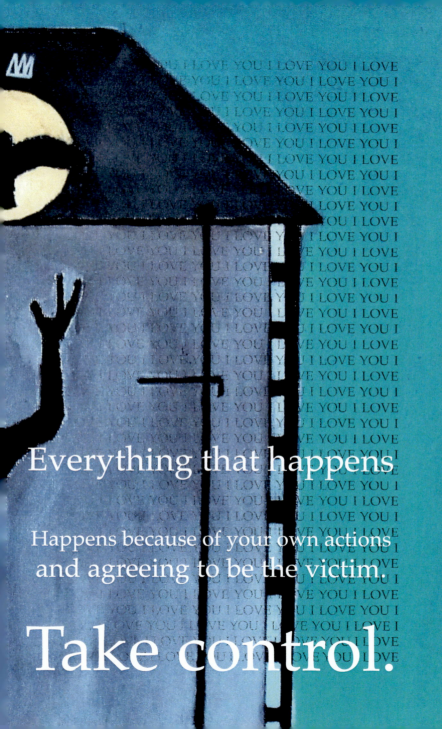

Everything that happens

Happens because of your own actions and agreeing to be the victim.

Take control.

v
i
n
g
a
m
o
m
e
n
t

JjusthavingamomentjusthamomT
U \justhavingamoment/ N
S \thavingamome/ E
T \sthavingamo/ M
H \havdealing/ O
A \einwitha/ M
V \myour / A
I \jshita/ G
N \ju/ N

_____

N /st\ N
G /havi\ I
A /ngamo\ V
M /mentjusth\ A
O /vingamoment\ H
M /jussthavingamo\ T
E /mentjusthavinga\ S
N /justhavingamoment\ U
TNEMO A GNIVAH TSUJ

m
o
m
e
n
t

The oldest living tree is a 3,000-year-old yew. Yew typically have a lifespan of about 400–600 years. They can grow so old because they can split under the weight of advanced growth. Most trees will succumb to disease after they split – but not the yew. The yew then gives rise to new shoots from breaks in the bark low on its trunk. It can do this at any point in its lifespan.

                    I
                    Just
                    Want weed gear eccy
                    You
                    To
        I can't Deal with it
                    With
                    Your
                    Shit
                    I
                    Just
                    Want weed gear eccy
                    You
                    To
        I can't Deal with it
                    With
                    Your
                    Shit

You sleep like actual babies do. Fitting. Grasping for a tit that isn't there. Breath tinny and rattling. I knew I could make my move by the sound of your teeth grinding. You are hugging a pillow. Chewing your thumb. Two more bottles have been added to the pile. It's strange how after just a night of sitting in your cupboard I no longer notice the stink.

```
DO NOT BE PARANOID
D                              D
O                              O
N        everyone             N
O        is looking at        O
T        you…                 T
B                              B
E        But don't let it     E
P        bother you.          P
A        Everyone is          A
R        looking at           R
A        everyone else        A
N        all the time.        N
O                              O
I            O                 I
D                              D
DO NOT BE PARANOID
```

```
HAHAHA        HAHAHA
     HA       HA
    HA       HA
     HA   HA
      HAHA
```

```
       HAHAHA          HAHAHA
            HA       HA
            HA       HA
            HA   HA
            HAHA
```

```
HAHAHA        HAHAHA
     HA       HA
    HA       HA
     HA   HA
      HAHA
```

```
HAHAHA          HAHAHA
      HA          HA
      HA          HA
      HA    HA
        HAHA


HAHAHA          HAHAHA
      HA          HA
      HA          HA
      HA    HA
        HAHA
```

I leave you sleeping. I walk out by the front door. I take the knife and carve BEAST in letters as big as I can manage. I post the knife through the letterbox. As I make the walk back to my mother's home, I stop off at our tree. The S for Sarah looks like a backward zed. I look up to see how all the branches have shot off in a thousand different directions, sprouting new leaves with new lives and second chances. Tonight, I will cut down the tree. I will build a funeral pyre. Sarah will burn. Zara will wake in the ashes. Tomorrow, I will take the bus back to Glasgow. I will never come back here.

LIT @ YAS

34. ZARA DRINKS A BOTTLE OF WINE IN A BUBBLE BATH

Hurt hurts when it's working too much.
Hurt hurts when it's borrowing money.
Hurt takes up all your time.
Hurt hurts when it's not texting back.
Hurt hurts when it's smoking too much weed.
Hurt hurts when it's drinking until it's sick.
Hurt hurts when it's afraid.
Hurt hurts when it thinks about cockroaches
Hurt hurts so bad it cannot sleep.
Hurt hurts when it misses misery.
Hurt hurts when it gets hard in the morning.
Hurt hurts when it smokes.
Hurt hurts the ones it loves.
Hurt heals when it cries.
Hurt heals when it realises it was wrong.
Hurt heals when it gets what it needs.

Those who have been hurt in turn hurt others.
Until all they can do is double down and repeat.
So hurt people hurt people until they scream

Hurt! People! Hurt! People! Hurt!
People! Hurt! People! Hurt! People!

35. SOMETHING THAT NEVER HAPPENED ;)

A play in the end of a book of poetry that's got a story in it.

SCENE
A nondescript office in Glasgow City Chambers.

CHARACTERS

MR. KING   A middle-aged CEO.
ZARA   A young businesswoman.
SPIKE   A Staffordshire bull terrier.

The actress who plays ZARA comes on stage accompanied by four stagehands who help her into her costume. She is dressed professionally. Her hair is tied into a tight unmoving bun. Zara sits in a waiting room. The walls are decorated with awards, photographs from opening nights and a painting of the Old Gorbals.

Zara pulls out a notebook. Squinting at the photographs and awards, she takes notes. A light affixed to the frame of Mr King's office door suddenly glows red.

BAW DEEP IN A STAFFY

MR KING: ZARA CHISOLM!

Zara lets herself through the door. As she enters an onstage curtain falls, revealing MR KING'S OFFICE. Compared with the grandeur of the waiting room, the office is remarkably plain. Zara takes a seat. Mr King is looking at his phone.

ZARA: Hello.

MR KING: Ah. Good morning. Apologies, I was just checking how the leather belts are doing.

ZARA: The leather belts?

MR KING: How are you?

ZARA: I am fine, Mr King.

MR KING: Excellent. As I am sure you will have guessed, the council have granted us planning permission to remodel the Merchant City as Glasgow's red light district.

ZARA: I am pleased. It is an historic opportunity for the company. A chance to remodel and regenerate a whole portion of the city – and build an entire industry from the ground up.

MR KING: At C1 we are a family. I see from your CV you have worked with us for four years. Tell us about some of your greatest challenges.

ZARA: In my tenure as bar manager for Shoogle I overcame a major PR disaster. Due to a design quirk in the building there was a two-way mirror into one of the toilets. An employee had been charging customers fifty pounds to use

ZARA (cont'd): the mirror to spy on other customers. Obviously the employee was put through the disciplinary process and then fired without a reference. Their identity was passed along to the authorities, and their conduct was reported to industry watchdogs. Some questions were raised in the press as to C1's commitment to the safety of women in our venues. However, as we had been operating a mixed-gender toilet policy since my appointment as bar manager it was rightly concluded that this unfortunate instance was the act of a lone opportunist and not representative of the company as a whole.

MR KING: What skills will you bring to this position?

ZARA: Since I turned 16 I have been working as a camgirl. To this day I still run a live webcam show. I tell tantalising stories and perform strip dance routines for a world-wide audience. While running this webcast I learned how to keep accounts of my business practices, the soft skills of sex work (such as active listening, effective communication and how to maintain control of a conversation). I also learned an important fact about sex work. 90% of the income comes from 10% of the customers. Thus it is more profitable to tailor services to a small network of committed customers. Once I had graduated I joined AdultWork and started a successful escorting service – gaining clients from London, Amsterdam and throughout the central belt of Scotland. But I realised that if I did not develop my skills my youthful advantage would quickly dissipate. When the Red Light District project was trailed in Glasgow, under your masterful supervision, I realised two things. First – that there was a chance for me to work in an industry I am passionate about with a company that has been very good to me. And second – there was an opportunity for me to perform large-scale grassroots market research that would put me head and shoulders above any candidate that had merely studied this business from an ivory tower.

MR KING: What football team do you support?

ZARA: Celtic.

MR KING: How much does a ticket cost?

Zara is blank faced. Her shoulders tense.

MR KING: This position requires an undergraduate degree. Looking at your CV I see you have no formal education beyond high school. I suppose that is the end of this interview.

ZARA: When I was 16 I enrolled at Stirling University.

MR KING: Oh?

ZARA: I completed two years of an undergraduate degree in Business Studies. I was awarded a HND for my time there.

MR KING: This is still below the level normally required for an interview.

ZARA: But you don't need another daft wee lassy with a diddy degree from Mickey Mouse Uni. Having said that - my time at Stirling was not wasted. There I learned the social niceties and graces that are the entry requirement to operating at this level of society.

MR KING: That's where you learned it, aye?

ZARA: Aye.

MR KING: What does your mother do?

ZARA: She's a nurse.

Mr King shoots her a look.

MR KING: Why do you think I need you?

ZARA: You have quite an impressive wall in the
                waiting room.

MR KING: Thank you.

ZARA: I was particularly drawn to the opening night
                photographs. Peace, Shoogle, G.O.L.F – the Red
                Light District. I was drawn to them by what is
                absent. Do you read poetry, Mr King?

MR KING: *(a lie)* Of course!

ZARA: Are you familiar with a painting titled The
                Poets' Pub? The painting features Norman
                MacCaig, Hugh MacDiarmid, Sorley Maclean,
                Iain Crichton Smith, George Mackay Brown,
                Sydney Goodsir Smith, Edwin Morgan and
                Robert Garioch in the foreground. In the
                background there is a faceless woman. That
                woman is Stella Cartwright. They called her, in
                her day, the Muse of Rose Street. All these great
                men relied on her: for her talk, her vision – and
                her insight. In every photo of every opening
                night – you stand alone. You need me because
                every king needs a queen.

MR KING: Thank you for coming today. We shall let you
                know in due course.

ZARA: That isn't good enough.

MR KING: I'm sorry?

ZARA: This meeting is a formality. You would not have
               let me in the door if you had not already
               decided on me.

MR KING: The responsibilities of your new role are thus:
               live your life. Do whatever pleases you. All day,
               all night. Attend lavish gatherings with me,
               work the crowd and leave everyone you meet
               with a smile on their face. Understand our
               business. Innovate it. If you want. Your
               expenses are unlimited. Your salary is whatever
               you want it to be. All you have to do is sign a
               contract that says you are mine in perpetuity.

ZARA: Get it out, then.

Mr King gestures off stage. He reaches into his desk and pulls
out a jar of peanut butter. A stagehand comes on stage with an
9-year-old boy wearing a Staffordshire bull terrier costume. This
is SPIKE.

MR KING: I knew a good man, once. Mr Spence. He was
               from The Drum. You won't remember this: but
               there was a time when the mere mention of
               such places conjured images of children with
               machetes and burnt out motors.

Mr King unzips his trousers. He opens the jar of peanut butter.

MR KING: Mr Spence was a solid man. A man of full
               measures. A long necked man. But he knew
               which side of the bread was getting buttered.
               He came to C1 looking for a job, and he got one.
               For the sake of his young family he worked,
               and saved, to get himself out of his situation.

Mr King takes a handful of peanut butter and lathers it on his testes.

MR KING: When C1 venues undertake renovation, we subcontract the work to smaller firms. We contact multiple parties and have them bid for the contract. This means, at the upper managerial level, a lot of bribes are taken.

Spike licks Mr King's testes.

MR KING: Mr Spence worked out his particular manager was on the take. Instead of going to the law, he confronted the man himself. Because John is a solid man. Mr Manager followed protocol. He offered Mr Spence 20 grand in a brown envelope to keep quiet.

Mr King masturbates.

MR KING: So MR SPENCE went two levels above his manager. For you see: his world view didn't allow for this sort of thing to happen. He believed what we had been selling him. A fair day's work for a fair day's pay. He thought he could blow a whistle and it would all go away. As if the problem was not endemic. As if the rot was in the hand rather than the heart.

Mr King slaps Spike in the face. He forces his head further down on his erection.

MR KING: Reality is damage control. Reality is a commodity. I own reality. I am the real in 'GET A REAL JOB'.

Mr King picks Spike up and places him on top of his desk. Mr King rubs peanut butter on his own erection.

MR KING: This is the truth, Zara. The world is fucked. It has always been fucked.

Mr King slides his penis into Spike's anus. He starts a steady rhythm.

MR KING   But after you realise this – you just have to pick yourself up and plod on. No one cares about your pain. No one cares how hard you have it. No one cares if you waste your precious life on feeling sorry for yourself.

Mr King's thrusts get deeper and harder. Spike yelps.

MR KING: All anyone really cares about is whether you can do the business. So you have to do what everyone else can't. You need to give everything 100%, and fuck every cunt along the way.

Mr King starts jack-rabbiting.

MR KING: STICK YOUR FINGER IN THE DOG'S MOUTH! THIS IS THE FUCKING WORLD WE LIVE IN NOW, ZARA. COME WITH ME. THIS IS THE FUCKING WORLD WE LIVE IN. EVERYONE IS TRAUMATISED. EVERYONE IS COMPLICIT. GOD IS DEAD AND EVERYTHING IS SEX. DO NOT CRY. NEVER CRY. PICK YOURSELF UP. DUST YOURSELF OFF. AND PLOD. THE FUCK. ON.

Mr King reaches orgasm.

MR KING: Charlie will send the full contract over tomorrow. Take some time to think this over.

ZARA: What happened to Mr Spence?

MR KING: He is a team leader in the Alloa branch of

MR KING   McDonalds. He has a nice house and 1.9
(cont'd)   wonderful children. He gains half a stone every
             two years.

Zara exits through the office door. The lights go down. Zara is
illuminated by the red light. She takes down Mr King's photos
and replaces them with her own.